ENZO TRISTON

LIVING WITH A GREEN HEART

The Essential Guide to Green Living, Discover
Helpful Ideas on How You Can Practice Greener
Living to Help The Environment

Descrierea CIP a Bibliotecii Naționale a României
ENZO TRISTON
   LIVING WITH A GREEN HEART. The Essential Guide to
Green Living, Discover Helpful Ideas on How You Can
Practice Greener Living to Help The Environment / Enzo
Triston – Bucharest: Editura My Ebook, 2021
   ISBN

ENZO TRISTON

LIVING WITH A GREEN HEART
The Essential Guide to Green Living, Discover Helpful Ideas on How You Can Practice Greener Living to Help The Environment

My Ebook Publishing House
Bucharest, 2021

CONTENTS

What is Green Living?

We hear a lot about green living on an almost daily basis, yet many people aren't aware of what those very important words are really all about. Green living, or living green as men refer to it as, is living your life in an environmentally responsible and eco friendly way in an attempt to decrease the ecological impact you'll make.

There are wide varieties of practices we can all take to conserve our resources and help keep our planet healthy. Some of the most common include sustainability, recycling, alternative energy sources, green construction, organic food choices and several other environmental topics.

Becoming educated on green living and its impact on the environment is the first step towards each of us doing our part because it has to be a group effort. If we all want our children and grandchildren to live healthier lives, it needs to start now with us and needs to continue. Your local library, government agencies and the Internet are great sources of knowledge and information about green living and the part it plays in decreasing global warming and preserving the planet.

Simple things can make a huge difference such as using organic flowers and plants for decorations as opposed to artificial flowers you buy in the supermarket. Instead of using batteries that need to be tossed in the garbage after a few weeks, consider rechargeable green batteries. The next time you consider buying a new item of clothing, consider recycling something you already own. Are you having invitations made up for your next big party? If so, consider making your invites on the computer and emailing them or using recycled paper.

These ideas may not seem like much, but they'll make a huge contribution to living green.

We can't be expected to change our lifestyles overnight and no one expects us to do so. However, by making just a few changes in our daily lives, and encouraging our children to do the same, we'll be making a huge impact on the problem of global warming. Rather than making huge changes in your lives, try adopting new methods of doing the same things. For instance, next time you go shopping for a snack, look for items that use recyclable packaging. We all like drinking water.

Rather than buying bottled water day after day, consider refilling the bottle a few times before tossing it. An even better idea is investing in a eco friendly stainless steel water bottle. You're still going to be drinking the water you love so much, but you'll be doing it in a green or eco friendly manner. These simple steps are what it's going to take to provide generations to come with a healthier environment.

Better Choices Make for Greener Living

Living green is all about making smart choices for ourselves and for your homes. It's not just something we do occasionally but a matter of taking action and making choices that will provide us with a more sustainable and healthier life 365 days a year. It's also something we all have to do. Choosing a green lifestyle can involve purchasing an energy efficient hybrid car or building an energy efficient home with solar and wind power. However, we don't have to go to these extremes to make the choice to live greener. We can do many small things in our daily lives that will help keep our environment greener and save our planet.

Wintertime is a difficult time for many with the cold weather and icy roads and sidewalks. Ice is often eliminated with the use of a salt. While salt quickly eliminates the ice and makes roadways and walkways easier, we seldom realize the damage these salts are doing to our environment. The

10

commercial salts you buy at your local hardware store have chemicals such as calcium chloride, sodium chloride, potassium chloride or magnesium chloride, which are toxic to trees, plants and waterways.

When the snow melts away, the salt is washed into our rivers and lakes. It only takes one teaspoon of this salt to permanently contaminate 5 gallons of water. The best way to eliminate this problem is to shovel or plow the snow before it has a chance to accumulate. If you must use deicers, choose ones that are salt free, biodegradable and have a low toxicity rate. Even when using these deicers, use them as lightly as possible.

Using compact fluorescent light bulbs is another way consumers can contribute to a greener lifestyle. Compact fluorescent light bulbs not only save almost 300 pounds of carbon dioxide a year but also use 60 percent less energy than conventional light bulbs. Compact fluorescent light bulbs rated as Energy Star are a great way to do your part for the planet. By replacing just one light bulb with a CFL will conserve enough energy to light up over 2.5 million homes for 365 days. It will also prevent greenhouse gases equal to the emissions of almost 800,000 cars. Just imagine if you replaced all the light bulbs in your home with Energy Start light bulbs!

Water is something we use every day and often take for granted. However, we seldom stop to consider the true value of water or the importance of conserving it. Simple measures you can do right inside your home to conserve water include using water saving showerheads, ultra low flow toilets and drip free faucets and filters.

Benefits of Buying Green Energy

We're constantly hearing or reading about the benefits of living greener lifestyles as an attempt to help save the planet. There are many ways we, as individuals, can do our part to save energy and help the environment from simply using recyclables to building solar powered homes. While many people think of powering their homes with green energy as a major step, it's actually one of the easiest ways to have a huge impact on global warming and the environment.

Green power is generated from nature in the form or renewable energy sources like the sun, wind, hydro and geothermal. Why should we continue to pay thousands of dollars each year in energy costs between heating, electricity, hot water, etc. when green energy is out there waiting? The benefits of switching to green energy are phenomenal.

Using green energy lessens, if not eliminates, CO2 byproducts, carbon dioxide, sulfur dioxide and other pollutants that result from the fossil fuels used to create energy. This is a huge benefit to the environment.

Because our natural resources are depleting faster than they can be replenished, we've had to purchase fossil fuels from other countries, accounting for billions of dollars spent each year. In 1997 alone, $65 billion dollars went to other countries to have fossil fuels imported here. By using more renewable energy resources right here in our country, we're keeping the money here to help economy and create more jobs.

The major difference between fossil fuels and the sun is that while the sun will last forever, oil will not; therefore, the future of our children relies on us using more renewable energy sources. Our country's dependency on foreign oil has put our freedom on shaky ground. Switching to renewable sources of energy will decrease that dependency.

Production of wind generated electricity has increased 31 percent last year as electricity supplies and utility companies are supplying the customer's demand for cleaner energy. Consider plugging into this rapidly growing division of the power energy. You'll not only enjoy cleaner air but will save thousands of dollars each year.

Buying clean energy really will make a financial difference in your wallet. Purchasing just one 100kWh block of renewable energy is as beneficial as not driving a car for 2400 miles. Power providers in some states such as Colorado are now offering their customers blocks of renewable energy. They can buy enough to cover their monthly bill or choose to buy just one or two blocks. Learning more about renewable energy for our homes is the first step towards a greener environment for everyone.

Green Appliances Really Can Make a Difference

Although appliances and electronic gadgets in our home seem to be something we cannot get along without, we seldom consider how much they're costing us in energy and money.

Unfortunately, so many consumers look for the least expensive appliance when it comes time to purchase one. With the emphasis on conserving energy and saving the planet, shoppers now have the choice of purchasing "green" or energy efficient appliances.

Consumers are now becoming more aware of the importance of having green appliances in their home and the differences they can make. By purchasing eco friendly appliances and utilizing them in an energy efficient manner, we can save money and our planet at the same time. It really does not get much better than that!

Whether you're building, renovating or just in need of new appliances, the time is perfect to create your green home with green appliances. You, as the owner of the appliances, are not the only one benefitting from purchasing green appliances and becoming environmentally conscious.

There are many types of green appliances now on the market today. Look for the Energy Star label and you know you're looking at energy efficient appliances. The average home in America spends from $1,300 to $1,900 annually in energy costs. However, they can save an average of 30 percent on their cost just by switching to Energy Star rated appliances. This can add up to many dollars in savings. Appliances that qualify for the Energy Star rating include refrigerators, stoves, dishwashers, window air conditioners, washing machines, dryers and dehumidifiers.

Energy Star appliances may seem more expensive at the time of purchase, but the savings consumers experience in water, sewer and utility bills more than makes it worth the cost.

Energy Star appliances use up to 50% less water and energy than conventional appliances. Appliances need to meet certain requirements to earn the Energy Star label. For instance, refrigerators must provide a savings of 20 percent while dishwashers should save approximately 41 percent.

The Energy Star program is designed to help homeowners and consumers save money on energy. Homeowners get a savings of $60 for every Federal dollar spent on this fabulous program. Purchasing Energy Star appliances does more than save you money on your energy costs. Many tax credits and rebates are offered to consumers making energy efficient improvements such as green appliances in their home.

The savings from everyone switching to green appliances would be phenomenal. In fact, if just one in every ten homes switches to Energy Star appliances, greenhouse gases would be affected almost as though they planted over 1.7 million acres of trees. By purchasing green appliances, you're not only saving your money but the environment as well.

Introducing Children to Living Green

We've all heard that living green is something that should be started at home. However, it needs to be started at a very young age. If suddenly at the age of twelve, you're throwing all these "going green" ideas at your children, they're not going to know what hit them. They're also not going to be in the habit of living green.

Living green can be started on the day of their birth. On second thought, it can be started before they're even born by creating a green nursery. No, I don't mean the entire nursery needs to be painted green. Here are some great and very easy tips on how to implement living green into your child's life from their first day in your home.

Cloth diapers are not only more helpful to the environment but are also better for your child. Almost all parents use wipes on their babies. Choose wipes that are chlorine free and are biodegradable. An even better choice is using a washcloth.

While it's great to dress your child in fancy new clothing, using secondhand clothing will help conserve material needed to make new clothing. Consider thrift shops, eBay or ask friends and relatives for clothing they're no longer using. They'll often be more than happy to make the extra space in their homes.

When choosing your baby's crib, look for a crib that can later be turned into a child's bed. If you're planning to paint the crib or bedroom furniture, make sure you use nontoxic paints. The same goes for toys, which should be made from wood or organic cotton. When choosing bedding, make sure you avoid materials that may contain and release volatile organic chemicals, also known as VOC, in the atmosphere.

If you're renovating the nursery, choose nature materials such as flooring of bamboo, solid wood, cork or organic cotton. If you're planning to use carpeting, choose wool carpets. Any of the soft furnishings for the nursery should be made from natural and organic fabrics. Although natural is good, organic is even better.

When it comes to cleaning either the nursery or your baby's clothing, choose cleaning solvents that are free from harmful chemicals. Try to use as many natural based products as possible. This includes fabric softeners. Consider hanging their clothing on the line. Few things will make their clothing smell and feel quite as fresh as the sun or wind from nature.

By starting your baby's life in a green nursery, you're not only helping the planet but giving your baby the best possible start in life.

Providing your Children with a Green Lifestyle

We're constantly hearing about living a greener lifestyle and ways of implementing it into our homes and into our children. The best way you can encourage your children to becoming interested in a greener life is through example.

Don't just tell you children they must live a green lifestyle. Set an example for them and explain the importance to them and everyone around them. Children are going to be more willing to try something new and different when they know the reasons behind it. However, if living green is something they've experienced since birth, they won't know any other way.

We've all heard the saying about families that play together stay together. At least it's my saying. Few things will make a young child happier than taking a walk with their parents or being allowed to go for a bike ride with their parents or siblings. Encourage your child to walk or ride a bike as much as possible at a very early age as opposed to hopping in the car and using fuel. If necessary and possible, consider showing them the advantages of using public transportation.

Children love helping their parents, especially when they're doing something with their parents as opposed to for them. Ask for their help with carrying buckets of kitchen waste out to the compost pile. Ask them to help you sort out the recyclables. Many children today earn an allowance for chores they do. Consider this part of their chores. Designate one evening per month for going around the neighborhood collecting cans and other trash.

Take your children to growers and farmer's markets where they can see that fruits and vegetables are not something that can only be found in the supermarket. If you have the space, consider growing a garden so they can see how produce is grown. They may not enjoy the weeding, but they'll sure enjoy the fresh produce. Consider letting them choose one or two items they can grow on their own in your garden. They'll love having their own project. Initiate a friendly competition in the family as to who can grow the healthiest produce.

Teach your child the importance of conserving at a young age. This may include limiting the number of toys they have as well as shutting off lights when they're not needed. Teach children the importance of not running the water steady when washing up or brushing their teeth. The green habits you teach your children at a young age are habits they'll take with them into adulthood.

Simple Step for Living in a Greener World

Hearing and reading about the need for us to go green is nothing new. It's been around for several years now; however, to many it's still a fairly unfamiliar and uncommon practice. So many people have the mistaken belief that the few changes they could make in their lives couldn't possibly make a difference. If they only realized that ten people each making small contributions to a greener way of life would make a huge impact on our environment.

Every year billions of U.S. dollars are going to other countries for the fossil fuels we need here for transportation and our homes. We are slowly depleting our resources at a pace that they cannot be replenished. Conserving energy in our homes is a very simple way we can help this problem. Turning off your lights when you're no longer in a room will save electricity in the same way as unplugging appliances that are not being used.

If you're going to be gone from your home for more than an hour, lower your thermostat. By making these simple yet smart eco friendly choices in your daily lives, our children and grandchildren will have a much greener and healthier tomorrow. In the spring and summer months, discontinue using your dryer and hang your laundry on the line. You'll save money, they'll smell fresh and you're helping the planet conserve energy and resources.

I remember many years ago hearing that leaving your television or radio on all the time made such a small difference that it wasn't even worth figuring. However, that was when utility costs were a fraction of what they are today and we weren't in danger not having the natural resources. Things have changed through the years and not for the better. However, we, as a group, can make things better once again.

You don't have to rush out and buy a new hybrid car or build a new solar powered home to make a difference. Try the simple steps I've mentioned above and see the difference in your utility bills the next month. Doesn't everyone want lower utility bills? The amount you save on your utility bills in a year can easily pay for a fantastic vacation for the family!

You don't have to live in the country to grow and enjoy fresh organic vegetables. Even if you live in the city, you can make a small garden and grow your own produce. Fresh vegetables are not only healthier and taste better, but they'll also help save resources. If you can't grow your own, consider buying your organic produce at the local grower or farmer's market.

Making Your Home More Green

Deciding to make the change to green living may be the best decision you'll ever make for yourself and your family. You've probably heard all about the importance of using natural, organic or eco friendly products, but may not be sure of what that all entails. Products that fit in this category are less toxic and less wasteful than conventional products, are environmentally friendly and safe for your home, your family and the entire environment. Sound complicated? It's actually easier than you think to make your home green.

As they say, Rome wasn't built in a day, and you're not going to turn your entire lifestyle and home green overnight, but you can make simple changes that make a huge difference. Whether you're choosing to go vegan, organic, buy all new energy efficient appliances or just concentrate on using less energy, you'll be making a great change in your life and the lives of those around you.

Cleaning takes up a large part of every day so the type of cleaners you're using is very important. When choosing cleaners, check if they're biodegradable, non toxic, contain petroleum distillates, and if the packaging is recyclable. A simple and healthy household cleaner you can make yourself is one quart of warm water and two teaspoons of white vinegar.

Bedding

We spend around one third of our life in bed, so make sure you're using bedding that's safe and eco friendly such as pillows and mattresses made of organic natural products. Linens made of 100 percent organic fibers will help you breath better at night and will not irritate your skin. In addition to being better for the environment, they do not contain harmful chemicals. For bedroom sets, select natural hardwood products.

Clothing

Did you know that each year over 80 million pounds of chemicals are used on conventional cotton farming? This process is highly toxic and harmful and pollutes the air, water, soil and our wildlife. The best choices you can make in clothing are those made with natural organic materials like hemp, organic cotton and reused materials. Hemp is not only extremely soft but very durable. I realize you don't want to nor can afford to buy a completely new wardrobe, but making gradual changes to eco friendly clothing can make a big difference.

Lighting

Have you ever stopped to consider how many hours of the day your lights are on in your home? I'm sure you've often wondered why your electric bill is so large. Consider greening your lights by switching to solar lights, skylights, low cost compact fluorescent bulbs and other natural sources of light. Keep your drapes open as long as possible to take advantage of the daylight hours.

Living Green Is Making Healthy Choices

When we hear the phrase living green, each of us have different images and opinions of what that entails. The reason is that there are so many ways we can all live green in our daily lives. Actually, living green is all about make Earth friendly, healthy choices that are good for your health as well as good for the environment. The healthy smart choices we make today will not only help us, but will help our children, grandchildren and generations to come.

When we're discussing living green, three words frequently come to mind: reduce, reuse and recycle. We can reduce in many ways, starting with reducing the amount of energy we consumer and reducing the amount of food and every day products we waste. Reusing involves using things that can be reused rather than tossing them in the trash and buying something new.

Everywhere we look, it seems we see people buying and drinking bottled water. Consider reusing the bottle or investing in an eco friendly stainless steel water bottle. They're lightweight and extremely durable. If you have good drinking water in your faucet, use it. Rather than packing your child's lunch in disposable plastic or paper lunch bags, use reusable containers. They're not only healthier but more cost effective as well.

Recycling is probably the most important thing we can do to live greener lives. So many things today can be recycled. When taking out the trash, take the time to sort it into groups of recyclables such as paper, plastic, etc. If you have to use batteries, use rechargeable batteries as a way to keep hazardous materials out of the landfills. When purchasing light bulbs, use compact fluorescent bulbs. While they may seem more costly at the time of purchase, they use about 25 percent of the energy of conventional bulbs and last 13 times longer.

Heating and electricity are two forms of energy that are used and abused more than anything else. You can conserve several ways on both of these energy sources. When you go to bed, lower your heat by a couple degrees, which will save more fuel than you'd imagine. In addition, lower the heat by at least

10 degrees if you're going to be gone all day. Why heat an empty house?

Turn off lights in rooms that are not being used. When you go to bed at night, all lights should be turned off. For outdoor lights, consider motion sensor lights that will only turn on when there is motion nearby and shut off when the motion is out of range. Appliances and electronics that are not being used should be unplugged. They continue to use energy when they're plugged in, whether they're actually turned on or not.

Lastly, always eat healthy. Making healthy food choices is a great way to not only live green but live healthy. Choose natural organic foods and always know what you're eating.

Living Green is Easier than You Think

We've all heard about green living and we all know what living green is all about. At least, most of us think we know what it's all about. What it's really all about is making eco friendly smart choices in the way we live our lives.

We've all heard the traditional methods of living green from turning off lights and lowering thermostats to buying hybrid cars and building green homes. We think either we can or cannot do it or are already implementing these green practices into our lives. Many of us live this way because we like to save money even without thinking about doing it for our planet.

Others, on the other hand, may think they're living green to the best of their abilities but are not making smart choices. In other words, their hearts are in the right places, but their heads are misinformed or have been mislead. Believe it or not, there are some Dos and Don'ts regarding effective ways to help the earth and live green.

Since we started using computers there's been the debate of whether to shut your computer off or leave it on when you're not using it. You're not going to be saving much if you're turning it off when you'll be using it again in 15 minutes. In fact, you may actually be doing more harm.

However, shutting it off for the night will make a big difference in your energy usage and the life of your monitor. Screensavers, unlike popular belief, do not save energy. If you won't be using your computer for 15 minutes or so, put it on sleep mode.

Switching the light bulbs in your home from conventional light bulbs to Energy Star compact fluorescent light bulbs is a great help to the environment and will also be a help to your pocketbook. These fantastic light bulbs last a very long time and will really cut down on your electric bill. However, wait until your current light bulbs are totally burnt out before replacing them. You'll be wasting money and energy replacing perfectly good bulbs. Make this transition one bulb at a time and you'll really be making a difference.

Have you been thinking of buying a hybrid SUV to reduce pollution and conserve fuel? SUVS are still gas guzzlers and not very economical. If you're serious about saving energy and fuel, you may want to consider a smaller car that's not a hybrid. It would almost make more sense than a hybrid SUV.

Yes, living green can mean growing green plants and trees in your backyard. However, unless you're really gung ho on the idea, skip the big lawn. While it may look pretty, it's going to require a lot of care including mowing (more gas and oil being used), herbicides, pesticides and lots of watering during the dry spells. If you are growing a garden, save your rainwater. It's an eco friendly way of living and will do wonders for your plants.

How Recycling Can Help Our Planet

We hear so much about the threat of global warming and ways we can help to save our planet. However, many people are under the impression that "saving the planet" is something far beyond the realm of what they can do on their own. Little do they realize that a simple thing like recycling can provide an enormous benefit to the planet.

Many believe that with the threat of something as serious as global warming hanging over our heads, something as simple as recycling can't possible make a difference. Just imagine if every individual developed a policy of recycle, reduce and reuse, what a powerful impact it would have on the planet as a whole. What exactly is recycling and how can it help?

Although recycling is a term we've just begun hearing more about the past decade, it's far from new as the Romans and Greeks implemented it as part of their daily life. Without even giving it a label, they were recycling. Once they discovered glass could be used over and over, they learned how to remake it. Quilts, curtains and clothing were salvaged and remade into new items. Waste was considered foolish and if something could be saved and remade into something else, it would happen.

The end of WWII brought about convenience-based economy and disposable items. While these disposals made our lives easier, they contributed to the landfills filling up. Now; however, the need to preserve and recycle is here. Unfortunately, much is still needed to be learned about recycling. It's about much more than crushing and saving our aluminum cans or bringing in our bottles to collect the deposit money.

For instance, many people do not realize that plastics can be recycled. Many of the reusable shopping bags and hiking socks we use today were plastic at one time. Items made of paper, aluminum and even glass can be used over and over before their life span is over. Recycling does not just save us all money, but it also saves energy and saves on our resources, which both are becoming depleted.

The idea of saving our paper and plastic items for recycling sounds easy enough. However, there are many other ways we can recycle to save our planet. When you're in the market for new appliances, don't just toss them in the garbage. Check in to any recycling programs you may have in your area.

Schools and many charitable organizations have a program where they collect old computers, DVD players and TVs and send them places where they can be refurbished. Our environmental health relies on us keeping the landfills free of electronics. There are actually few things that cannot be recycled. As group, we can all do our part to help our planet by finding recycling programs in our area.

Driving Your Way to a Green Future

Advancements in technology have brought us many new "green" products, but the things that are making the news the most are the new energy efficient hybrid cars. While hybrid cars may be more expensive at the time of purchase, which dissuades many consumers, the savings you'll experience in fuel consumption may make you decide that they're worth the cost.

Combine that with the bonus they provide to the environment and you'll see why so many car owners are choosing hybrids.

A hybrid car is one that uses one more one type of fuel, with the most common using gasoline and electricity. The electricity in the car is supplied by a very sophisticated battery system, although most hybrids run mostly on gasoline. The battery gets charged up by the gasoline or petrol motor and, in turn, powers some of the car's motion to provide you with better fuel economy.

With President Obama's Stimulus Bill, hybrids and electric cars are becoming more popular. The government has committed to billions of dollars to help develop these electric and hybrid cars to help with climate change and fuel economy with the price of oil fluctuating.

The most common type of hybrid car, known as a *parallel hybrid*, gets its transmission power from the internal combustion engine and the electric engine. Some full hybrids can run on just gas, just battery or a combination of both, although they're run only a limited time on the battery alone.

The Toyota Prius is full hybrid of this type, while the Honda Insight is an example of a *series hybrid*. This is a car where the electric part of the motor compliments the gasoline engine, providing you with excellent fuel economy. On the Honda Civic hybrid, the gas part of the car gives power to the generator, which supplies the electricity needed to run the motor.

Plug in hybrids are another energy efficient car used by consumers wanting to go green and save money at the same time. You plug them to charge them up as you would with a battery operated appliance. This allows the driver to use the car on battery mode for a longer time. One reason why plug in hybrids are so popular is because not only are they clean but also become cleaner with time. The reason is that the power stations, which provide the electricity, are becoming greener and cleaner each year.

While hybrid cars are still very new to many consumers, it's believed and hoped that when consumers see how economical and clean they are for the environment, they'll become the car of choice.

Make Your Next Party a Green Party

It seems like every time we turn around some sort of party is right around the corner. Whether it's an anniversary, birthday, shower or some holiday, there always seems to be some party about to happen. You've been doing as much as possible to maintain an environmentally friendly lifestyle so why not implement this aspect into your next party. There are several ways you can have a green party that will not only be spectacular as always but show your love for the planet to others as well.

Invitations are always the first part of any party. Once you've determined how many guests to invite, you head either to the local printing shop or to your computer and printer. Cutting back on the invitations you print can be a great first start towards your green party. Almost everyone today has and uses their email regularly. With the many word processing and card programs available, you can make attractive invitations and send them via email.

If, for some reason, you prefer to send out printed invitations, using post consumer, recycled paper. If you're sending out formal invitations such as for a wedding, eliminate the extra sheets that are often found in commercial wedding invitations. It's a waste of paper and the recipients just toss them in the trash.

I prefer to receive an invitation by email, where it's then put in a special folder for family or friends. At any given time, I can go look at it to double check the date and time. Almost all email programs have calendars with reminders so you won't forget about the party. Invitations I've received in the mail tend to be misplaced in my home at times.

Food is usually the next thing on your party agenda. Regardless of whether your party is in your home or at a restaurant or hotel, choose local organic food. While not all caterers use organic foods, many of them will use organic ingredients you give them, particularly if they want your business. You will not only be doing your part for the environment, but will also be providing your guests with delicious tasting food.

Most parties have decorations of some kind. Instead of buying artificial invitations, use natural ones such as garden or potted plants. You may also choose to give your guests one to take home with them. If you really want to use fresh flowers, put them in the compost pile after your party. Candles are very popular decorations today and many shops sell candles made with substances that are eco friendly.

Consider giving out and asking for green gifts. There are many choices available including theatre tickets, gift cards to restaurants offering local cuisine, artwork and more. If you're using a gift registry, look for green items.

Going Green in the Classroom

Going green is something that should take place in every part of our lives. It should be part of our daily routine – something we do without evening thinking twice. It should start at home with your family. Children that grow up in an environmentally friendly home become adults that are concerned with saving the planet for every generation to come. Once children reach school age, their habits will carry with them into the classroom, where the "save the planet" principles should continue.

There are several ways teachers can not only encourage students to go green but can also make it fun. A recycling program right inside the classroom will have all the students participating in the program. It doesn't have to be anything extraordinary or complicated.

Teachers can set up different boxes or compost bins for the trash and recyclables in the classroom.

For instance, you can have a green compost bin for food waste, blue box for recyclable paper and clear bags for juice boxes and similar items students may have. Besides the obvious benefits of a recycling program (helping the environment), this also gives students a better understanding of just how much garbage they're actually helping to keep out of our landfills.

Planting and gardening is something children have enjoyed since the beginning of time. If the school is located on property with sufficient room to plant trees, this is a great way to teach children the importance of keeping trees and other plant life growing. Many landscaping and garden companies will donate trees to schools participating in a recycling program.

Another way to encourage tree planting to children is by having them plant a small tree for their parents for Mother's or Father's Day. Knowing that they're helping the planet as well as making a gift for their parents is a great way to provide motivation, encouragement and excitement for the children. Town or city councils often offer young trees to schools for a very low fee.

The best part of any school day is always the time spent outdoors. Teachers can initial a nature way and combine it with a cleanup of the neighborhood. While they're outdoors enjoying the fresh air and sunshine they can also be filling recycling and trash bags with the garbage they see lying on the streets, sidewalks and roadways.

The most effective way teachers can encourage interest in recycling and conserving energy is by having open discussions in the classroom on global warming, recycling and the condition of the planet and environment for future generations and us. Encourage students to freely ask questions.

Recycling Paper for Greener Living

With all the things we hear on the news or in newspapers and magazines about recycling for greener living, many question just how important it is to recycle paper. Most people are more willing to put something into practice when they're aware of why they're actually doing it. After all, we all want to do our part to save our planet, but how exactly are our landfills being helped by us recycling paper? This is a question asked by many people.

The surest way for waste to develop in any situation is when we have a huge supply of it. This is definitely the case with paper. In the past 20 years, the consumption of paper has doubled in the United States. Any time the consumption of something increases, so does the amount of waste, which is the case with paper. In fact, paper makes up about one-third of our household waste.

Think about it once.

Newspapers, paper bags, old mail, magazines are all paper that is tossed in the trash. Newspaper alone fills up 14 percent of the space in landfills. So, therefore, eliminating or at least slowing down the speed that paper gets into our landfills will slow down the speed at which are landfills become full.

Decomposing paper in landfills is harmful to us as well. When paper is decomposed in landfills, methane gas is released. This greenhouse gas, which contributes to global warming, has 20 times the potency of carbon dioxide. Again, eliminating the amount of paper that gets into landfills, by recycling, can help the environment from global warming.

Saving energy is another way we can save the planet and live greener longer. It takes a lot more energy to make paper with virgin materials (from 28 to 70 percent) than it takes to recycle paper. For one thing, when paper is recycled, it seldom requires re-bleaching, which means fewer harmful chemicals are going in the air and atmosphere. When they do need to bleach it, they use oxygen instead of chlorine.

Have you ever heard people say they recycle paper to save the trees? This is actually a misconception. Today most paper comes either from trees grown specifically for paper or from sustainable wood supplies. As soon as the trees are harvested, new ones are planted to replace them. Parts of the tree that is unusable by many industries also often go into the making of paper. However, a certain amount of virgin wood does need to be used in making paper so we'll always need trees if we want paper. This is why it's so important to not only conserve our paper use, recycle it and continue to purchase recycled paper.

Tax Deductions for Living Green

We've all heard the many important reasons for living green. Our planet is in danger from the threat of global warming. Our natural resources are slowly being depleted from being used at a faster rate than they can be replenished. The harmful gas emissions coming from the millions of cars on the road today are slowly killing the atmosphere. Too many years of wasting energy and products has taken its toll on the environment.

We've all heard enough reasons to start implementing green living into our lifestyles. If these reasons aren't enough, how about the tax credits the government is giving for living green? We all like getting credit and tax breaks, and what better way than for doing something that's good for us and the environment? Here are just a few of the tax credits or breaks you can get by making a few green changes in your life.

Driving Can Earn You Credit

Driving your car every day can use up a lot of fuel, especially if you're traveling a great distance. The more you travel, the more harmful gas emissions coming out of your exhaust as well. Good news for car owners that purchase hybrid cars, as they're eligible for energy tax credits.

Owners purchasing plug in vehicles are also getting a tax break in the form of credits. Although the credit for hybrids is decreasing, electric cars are increasing. What could be better than getting better gas mileage plus credit from the government?

Savings in the Home

In spite of what you may believe, you don't need to rush out and install a new solar system in your home to be eligible for energy efficient tax credits. Simple upgrades inside your home will do that, providing you're upgrading to a new energy efficient model such as air conditioning unit, heating system, hot water heater, appliances, etc. The credit is based on 30 percent of the cost of the item up to $1,500 every two years.

Appliances; however, are not the only way you can earn these tax credits. Other upgrades include qualifying roof with skylights or parts that reflect the sun, weather stripping and insulation may qualify you for these credits.

Take the extra time to check out your local tax credit office for detailed information. Some areas offer credits for energy efficient printers, scanners, computers, and even televisions. Energy efficient ceiling fans will also get residents of certain states a tax credit as well as switching to energy efficient fluorescent bulbs.

If you're planning to make some improvements in the coming year, it may be beneficial to check out which products will garnish you some extra money in your pocket. Save the environment and save money. It's a win win situation for everyone.

Using Green Bags for Greener Living

All across the USA, we're hearing about the importance of reducing the use of paper and plastic shopping bags because of their negative effect on the environment. Individuals and businesses are choosing environmentally friendly shopping bags.

Green bags, also known as eco friendly bags, are not just a shopping bag that's green in color, but a specific style of bag designed to help you protect your family and the earth. Just what's so special about the new green bags that are being sold everywhere?

- Green bags can hold up to 22 pounds more than plastic shopping bags.

- Green bags are 100 percent recyclable, making them extremely eco friendly.

- Green bags will last up to two years or more, more than twice as long as plastic bags.

- Green bags have comfortable handles for carrying with your hands or on shoulder.

- Green bags are an oil derived product.

- Green bags, offered in many stylish colors, are washable.

- Green bags comply with FDA regulations.

- Green bags are made with dyes that are both colorfast and not harmful.

- Green bags are very durable.

- Green bags contain no toxic materials that could be harmful or allergenic to the skin.

There are many wonderful things to be said about green bags. In addition to being eco friendly, they're extremely attractive and convenient. On the way to the store, they can be easily folded and stored in your purse or handbag. They're also a very cost effective method of doing your part to save the planet.

Making the green bags is a very simple and effective process. They are mad from non woven polypropylene, which can also be recycled. The polypropylene is mixed with color pellets at a high temperature, cooled, then pushed through a machine that rolls out the fabric. Almost no greenhouse gas emissions go into the product of the green bags.

Because they can be made in a variety of lengths and widths, there is seldom any waste. Added to the benefits of using recyclable polypropylene is that if a bad batch of green bags are made, they can be shredded and reused into other products such as concrete items. Green bags made of non woven polypropylene are water repellent so there is no chance of odors or bacteria developing on or in the bags.

Shoppers that buy green bags are not only helping to save their planet, but are making a purchase that will add to their convenience and save money.

Snacking Your Way to a Greener Planet

Most of us snack on a daily basis, but how many of us are actually helping the planet when we do so? People that are purchasing and snacking SunChips are doing their part to help the planet almost as much as the manufacturers of SunChips have done. In addition to providing consumers with a product that's healthy, they've also providing packaging that's eco friendly.

We all dream of a world that has less waste, but few companies go to suchmeasures to actually do something about it quite like SunChips. In creating a bag that's made from plants, they managed to make a bag that's fully compostable. When the bag of SunChips is empty (doesn't take long since they're so delicious), the bag can be tossed in a hot, active compost pile or bin, where Mother Nature begins working. In approximately 14 weeks, the average 10 ounce SunChips bag is completely broken down.

If you've tried their new eco friendly packaging, you may notice that they're somewhat louder than their previous bags. This difference in sound is because the material is plant based. It doesn't take consumers long to get used to the sound, especially when they realize the positive impact they're having on the environment.

SunChips did long and detailed testing indoors and outdoors to develop this unique green bag. Their testing was done to ensure its strength, durability and mostly its compostability. The result was an amazing bag that's totally recyclable and compostable. Has this helped their sales? I can only imagine how many more consumers are buying SunChips today and enjoying snacking their way to a greener planet.

SunChips didn't just stop with their new packaging. They are very serious about doing their part for the earth. With all the hype today about solar energy, they couldn't imagine why they hadn't thought of this idea sooner. After all, the very name of their product is Sun Chips so why not use the sun in their process. Instead of using conventional fossil fuel in their Modesto, California plant, they started using solar energy.

SunChips discovered a way to capture the sun's rays as energy. Rather than waste this precious form of energy, they put it to good use. With the help of solar collectors, the sun is tracked from dawn to dusk, where it is then transferred into heat. The sun they manage to collect each day helps them to make 145,000 bags of delicious and popular SunChips.

Therefore, next time you're snacking on a bag of SunChips, be happy that you're not only eating something that's good for you but good for the planet as well.

Greener Ideas to Make for a Greener World

While we hear so much today about living green to help our planet and live healthier and more energy efficient lives, we seldom stop to think of the little things we can do to help the cause. While some may be practicing green living for the sole purpose of helping the planet, others may be doing it to save money. There are still others that live green because they feel it is providing them and their family with a healthier lifestyle.

Living green can help all those causes. While one method of green living may not appear to have an overall effect on the planet, it will provide healthier living or may save money. Living green is a complete cycle that involves making a lot of smart and eco friendly choices daily. For instance, did you know that if one out of every 10 homes used energy efficient appliances, it would be equivalent to planting 1.7 million acres of trees?

Green living such as this is saving money in the home and helping the planet. If it's helping the planet, it's providing us with a healthier life. It all works together and benefits everyone.

With the high cost of home remodeling, many homeowners are choosing to give their homes or rooms a quick facelift with a new coat of paint. Choose paint that is either low or zero VOC paint, otherwise, you may be using paints with toxic metals and solvents that will cause pollution and smog.

If you're planting trees or plants to beautiful your front or back yard, consider getting native plants. They have several benefits including their easy adaptability to the environment, require less attention, require less water, and you'll be supporting native animals as well.

If you have a dishwasher, be sure to use eco friendly soap. Do you rinse your dishes off before you put them in the dishwasher? If you are, you're not only wasting time, but you're wasting water as well. Dishwashers have heaters inside of them that boil the water to sterile your dishes. If your dishes need to be rinsed for the dishwasher to get them clean, it may be time for a new energy efficient dishwasher.

If the water from your washing machine is just draining outside, consider putting a bucket there and collecting it. It will work great in the garden to kill the weeds, provided you're using eco friendly detergent and soap.

The less paper we use in our daily lives, the more trees we're able to save. Post consumer recycled paper (it's also tree free) is used in all sorts of paper products including toilet paper, greeting cards and everyday copy paper. Did you know that you can save 52 pounds of solid waste, 584 pounds of wood and the water required for 50 eight minute long showers by using just one box of this post consumer recycled paper?

Green Living to Lower Your Energy Bill

We've all been told the importance of green living to help the environment and save the planet from the threat of global warming. However, the wonderful thing about living green is that we're not only saving the planet, but we can save money doing it. None us like opening up our utility bills only to discover it's higher than the month before and the winter months are yet to come!

The bottom line is when you're saving energy; you're saving resources, which will save you money. Saving money on your electric bill can be easier than you think. Even if you think you've been doing everything possible to lower your bills, I'll be willing to be there are still little things you may have overlooked.

In the process of looking for ways to lower the bill, you're probably coming across many things that you were told by your parent as you were growing up. They really did know what they were talking about! Here are some great tips on ways green living will help you lower you energy usage and costs.

- ***Light bulbs really will make a difference***. Switch from conventional incandescent bulbs to energy efficient compact fluorescent bulbs. For instance, using a 6 watt LED instead of a traditional 60 watt bulb can save you $280 over the life of the bulb. Imagine if you replaced all your bulbs with energy efficient ones.

- ***Lower your thermostat***. Since 50 percent of our home's energy costs come from heating and cooling, you can save $180 annually by lowering the temperature by two degrees. In cold weather, 3 to 5 percent energy can be saved for each degree under 68 degrees.

- ***Watch your water usage***. You can decrease your water usage in half by using an aerator on all your faucets. You can also save over 4 gallons of water by brushing your teeth without the water running.

- ***Get rid of that old refrigerator*** in the garage or basement and you can save up to $150 a year in energy costs. If you really are in need of a second refrigerator, buy an Energy Star appliance.

- *Use compost in your garden instead of commercial fertilizer*. Instead of throwing out all your scraps, start your own compost pile. You'll save money and your produce will thank you for the effort.

- *Choose bamboo flooring* as opposed to hardwood floors as it takes a lot less time for bamboo to mature than it does for the hardwoods used in flooring, and bamboo is more economical

Buying a Home While Going Green

In spite of how tough the housing market has been of late, many people are still looking for homes to buy. Whether you're a first time homebuyer or have done it before, it's important to remember this will be one of the biggest purchases and decisions you'll ever make. It's also a great opportunity to put your desire for a greener lifestyle into play by paying particular attention to the size, style and location of your home.

Ask for help from the realtors in finding home with good home energy performance. With the increased eco-awareness along with high energy costs, realtors are used to having consumers ask about greener homes and environmental issues surrounding these homes.

Hire a professional to do an energy audit on any home you're considering buying. An audit will tell you how efficient the home is and any upgrades it may need to become more efficient. You can check certain things yourself like the heating and cooling system, the condition of the windows and doors and insulation, but an auditor can give you facts that are more important.

It really is all about location when it comes to home buying. Take your place of employment into consideration. While you may love country living, are you going to have to spend a lot of time and money for commuting every day?

While we all love the idea of having a large home, we don't always like heating and cooling it so think small when looking at homes. Implement so unique furniture arrangements and decorating tips to make the most out of the space you have. The more space you have, the more you'll have to heat and cool.

Look over the home very carefully. While some green changes are going to be relatively easy and inexpensive, others are not. For instance, it's not too difficult or costly to apply a fresh coat of low VOC paint, which decorates your home. However, ripping out room after room of carpeting and refinishing the hardwood floors underneath may be more than you care to do.

If you're looking at older homes and are already planning on green renovations, look for homes that require the most renovation in the kitchen and bathroom, which are the two rooms where you'll get the most bang for your buck in terms of renovating dollars.

Check into the possibility of generating your own power in your potential new home. While it may not be something you can afford right at this moment, it will beneficial in the future to know it's possible. Check with your state officials on any rebates offered for energy efficient homes and using renewable energy.

Whether you're a tree hugger or not, trees are good for shade in the summer and letting natural light and heat into your home in the winter. They also provide a home for birds, which are great for the organic garden you're planning to grown. While you're checking out the yard, make sure there is enough room to grow a garden as well as build your compost pile.

Green Living Inside Your Home to Save Energy and Money

Green living doesn't have to mean building a new solar powered home or buying a new hybrid car. While these are both measures would save you a lot more through the years and help the environment, there are small steps you can take right inside your home to help save both energy and money. Green living, after all, should start right in your home and should involve the whole family.

We use and waste a lot of energy in our homes. Have you ever wondered where all the energy is used in our homes? Knowing where your energy is going may make it easier to decrease the amount of energy you and your family use each day. Here is a simple break down of the energy use in an average home.

- 34 percent: Lights and appliances
- 34 percent: Space heating

- 13 percent: Water heating
- 11 percent: Electric air conditioning
- 8 percent: Refrigerator

You don't need to buy expensive household cleaners that may be filled with toxins. There are items you probably have right in your home that will do the job just as well and will provide your family with a healthier environment. A mixture of one half cup Borax to one cup of fresh lemon juice works great as a toilet cleaner.

Vinegar seems to be a great all around household cleaner. Whether it's carpets, mirrors, windows or clogged drains, vinegar seems to serve many purposes. Straight vinegar works great on pet stains on your carpet while an equal mixture of vinegar and water will have your windows and mirrors shining. Vinegar also works well when mixed with your fabric softener.

Here are some simple tips on how you can save energy in your home.

- Use fluorescent bulbs rather than conventional light bulbs.
- Make sure your home is well insulated as well as your water heater.

- Turn your thermostat down at night and when you're gone. Use a programmable thermostat.
- Replace the filter on your furnace once a month in the winter.
- Make sure the coil on your refrigerator is clean so it will have to work less to keep cool. Make sure the gasket is clean as well.
- When doing laundry, make sure you have a full load and use warm water for washing and cold for rinsing. When possible, hang laundry outside to dry.
- When cooking, put lids on the pots and shut your oven off 15 minutes early.
- Thaw your food before cooking it.
- Let dishes in the dishwasher air dry.
- Collect rainwater for watering your plants.

Sending Your Children to School
with Green Supplies

Today we're hearing about the importance of living a green lifestyle more and more. With the threat of global warming hanging over our heads, it's more important than ever that we all try to do our part to help our planet stay healthy and green. We have many ways to contribute including cutting back on the amount of energy we use, recycling our waste and only using recyclable products just to name a few.

While we've tried very hard to educate our children on the importance of living green, we don't always have control over what they do when they're out of our sight such as in school. You may not have much control over what takes place in school, but by sending them to school with green supplies, you're encouraging them and others to continue your practice.

Make the same commitment to send your child to school with eco friendly supplies as you use right in your home. This may include their school supplies as well as lunch and snack items you provide them with when they leave each day.

Calculators are used by students of almost all ages, so you may as well get them a solar powered model as opposed to one that will continue to use batteries. Batteries are extremely bad in landfills and to the environment in general. Avoid using any products that use batteries unless it's unavoidable.

There seems to be no end to the amount of notebooks and paper they're going to use in a school year. Shop where they sell post consumer recycled paper. With the high interest we all seem to be taking in eco friendly products, you should be able to find this type of paper in most stores that carry school supplies. Markers, crayons and glue should all be nontoxic and as natural as possible.

There is more to the school day than just the time they're working. You don't want to forget about lunch and snack times. While it's important to provide them with snacks that are healthy, natural or organic, care should also be taken in the containers you use to send them in. Replace paper lunch bags or disposable plastic bags with reusable containers. Many of them will actually keep the food tasting better longer.

Plastic water bottles may be convenient and lightweight but also can pollute the liquids with chemicals over time.

Consider investing in child friendly stainless steel beverage containers. A good choice of snacks includes fresh fruits and veggies, homemade muffins and cookies made from low fat recipes and low fat dips. SunChips is a great snack choice because they're healthy, are made with solar energy and are packaged in eco friendly compostable bags.

Transportation Tips to Ensure a Greener Life

Transportation is a big part of our lives. We always seem to be going somewhere. We're driving to school, to work, visiting friends or driving some place for entertainment purposes. Regardless of what our goal may be, we are generally driving there. We just take for granted that we're going to be driving to our destination. Have you ever considered walking or biking if it's a short distance? Has the idea of occasionally taking public transportation ever crossed your mind?

You'd also be surprised how many benefits there are to carpooling.

In a recent study done by NASA's Goddard Institute for Space Studies, on road transportation was identified as the largest overall contributing source to global warming. Cars, trucks and buses are all major contributors as they release greenhouse gases and pollutants that promote warming while also not emitting enough aerosols to counteract it. The more vehicles on the roadways, the worse the problem of global warming is going to be.

While certain types of transportation can't be avoided, we can all pitch in to do our part in lessening this problem. Often simple steps are all that's needed because many simple steps add up to large results. If we all stopped to calculate the miles we drive in a week, or even a month, and figures out how much we're polluting the air, we would be amazed!

Many people don't understand how taking public transportation can help with the global warming problem when buses are emitting the same harmful gases and pollutants as our cars. The buses are going to be on the highways and roadways anyways. If ten people took the bus to work as opposed to driving their cars, there are ten fewer cars on the road. Which scenario is going to be more harmful to the atmosphere: a bus and ten cars or just a bus? It's a simple step that can make a lot of sense and a huge difference in our world.

Approximately 500 pounds of carbon dioxide emissions would be eliminated each year if 10 miles of driving were eliminated per week. By carpooling just two days each week, you'll be reducing the amount of carbon dioxide emissions each year by 1,590. As you can see, we don't have to make huge changes in our lifestyle to still be able to make a difference in the world we live in. Here are some very simple steps we can all take to decrease the amount of global warming contributed from transportation on the highways and roadways:

- Carpool to work with friends or family members.
- Consider taking public transportation once or twice a week.
- Walk or bike on trips less than 2 miles
- Invest in an energy efficient or hybrid car.

Benefits of Green Living

People everywhere are making a commitment to save energy any way they can, reduce waste and provide a healthier environment. They are doing this by living green. Living green is a concept that involves creating green homes, which are homes with energy efficient appliances and energy sources.

Homeowners are not the only ones that are benefitting from living green Communities, families and the world in general are all reaping the benefits of consumers being fiscally responsible and environmentally conscious. The more green homes we see the less waste we'll see in the landfills and the less we'll all be paying in energy costs. Water usage can be reduced by up to 50 percent and energy usage up to 60 percent less with the construction of a green home.

There are many benefits to living green. Economic Benefits

Many consumers see the initial cost of green homes and assume they are much more expensive than conventional homes. While they may seem more expensive at first, the savings they experience in the future more than makes up the difference. Green homes use less energy, require fewer repairs because of more durable building materials and provide lower energy costs.. Many insurance companies will charge lower premiums for green homes. The government has offered several tax breaks and rebates to those owning or buying green homes. There are savings all the way around when you go green in your home.

Health Benefits

Green homes can eliminate health issues from poor quality air often found in older homes by using non-volatile organic and non-toxic materials. Many people that previous suffered from respiratory discovered their breathing was much better when they started living green. When home materials are made with natural ingredients, there is also going to be less mildew or mold developing in the home. Breathing is also much easier because the natural ventilation systems replace the stale indoor air with fresh clean outdoor air.

Environmental Benefits

We've already heard about the small energy bills you'll experience due to less energy usage as well as the many health benefits of having a green home. What we didn't mention, which is probably one of the most important reasons for living green, is the benefit to our environment. When we use alternative or natural energy sources such as the wind, sun, biomass and geothermal energy, it reduces our dependence of fossil fuels and other conventional energy sources. We will no longer have to send billions of dollars to other countries for fossil fuel because our own supply is depleted. There really isn't a good reason to NOT live green in every way we can.

Printed by Libri Plureos GmbH in Hamburg, Germany